Fairy Tales Made Real

For Technical Enthusiasts

Dinesh Verma

Chanda Books

Email: chandabooks@optonline.net

Web: http://www.chandabooks.com

Preface

When I was a kid growing up in small factory town in India, one of the few entertainment options were the week-end movies screened by the factory club, which would feature popular Bollywood movies of the era. My first memory of those movies is a scene from a mystery movie which dealt with ghosts.

In the opening scene of the movie, the young dashing hero was driving alone in a car on a desolate road, when he encountered and picked up a mysterious women hitchhiker who asked to be dropped off near an old dilapidated house. The rusted gates of the old scary house open automatically as the woman approached and the audience let out a collective gasp. In that instant, the hero (and the audience) realized that the woman was not a normal person but a witch or a ghost.

Fast forward a few years, when I landed in the U.S. as a graduate student, and went to my first purchase at a grocery store in California. The somewhat dilapidated doors of the grocery store opened with a creak just as I stepped in front of them. For some reason, it triggered a flashback to that scary movie scheme. It is quite likely that the Bollywood movie copied or was inspired by a similar scene from some Hollywood movie. In a couple of decades (or maybe three or four), what used to be an indication of magic and witchcraft became a wide-spread phenomenon. Doors that open automatically are taken for granted today.

Ever since that, I have wondered how many other fairy tales and magical objects from the world of fantasy and mythology can be attained by technology. With advances in the power of computers, algorithms, and the ability to embed cheap powerful processors in every object, the set of magical objects that can be implemented technically becomes larger every day.

This book is a list of some of the fairy tales which can become real with modern technology. The magical objects in those tales can be recreated today, if one wants to invest sufficient time and money for this purpose. Recent advances in computers, artificial intelligence, ubiquitous connectivity, Internet of Things and other general technical advances are the ones that have enabled the magic to become real.

Since some of the fairy tales in popular use

today may be as old as 4000^{1} years, even the technology invented a couple of hundred years ago could have created the magical objects in these tales.

There are some magical things that are still beyond the reach of current technology (at least I can't think of a way to attain them practically). Examples include shape-shifting or transformation of humans into animals, or instant teleportation. While teleportation of really microscopic objects like photons has been shown as a possibility, there is no known practical technique to enable teleportation of any reasonable-sized physical objects – we don't even know a way to transport a grain of rice today. Of course, it does not mean that such technology may not be invented some day in the future.

Despite the existence of a few magical objects that are not feasible today, many are indeed technically viable. While they may not exactly be available in the supermarket next door, we can easily envision how to make that with the technologies we have at our disposal

---

[1] Sara Graça Da Silva, and Jamshid J. Tehrani. "Comparative phylogenetic analyses uncover the ancient roots of Indo-European folktales." Royal Society open science 3.1 (2016): 150645.

today.

One point to note is the fact that the technical feasibility of attaining a magical object does not really mean that it is commercially worthwhile to create that magical object, or that the object is common place at the present time. Technical feasibility means we can create the magical object, but it does not guarantee that the magical object is a worthwhile business investment.

Most of the ideas on how to create the magical objects are my opinions on how that magical object, or how something close enough to it can be created using modern technology, and without breaking the laws of Physics. While I have presented one approach, there are many alternative technical approaches that can be used for the same magical object. I would not claim that the approach presented in this book is the best possible way to create that magic object – rather it is just one feasible way, and the readers may be able to design a better way.

Another disclaimer is that this book only presents a high level approach to creating that magical object. The high level approach is written so that anyone with a high school science education would be able to understand it. This does not provide a detailed recipe that can be blindly followed to create the object.

Also, when those objects will actually be prototyped, they are very likely to lack complete fidelity to the actual magical object.

The fairy tales in this book are drawn from many different sources. Fairy tales have been shared across cultures, and many magical objects appear in more than one fairy tale. The book could have been organized with each chapter discussing a magical object, or each chapter discussing a fairy tale. I have taken the approach of discussing a fairy tale in each chapter, but it could have been equally organized in the other way.

Each chapter in this book provides a brief synopsis of the fairy tale or legend, a summary of the magical objects in that tale, followed by a discussion on how to create that magical object. The set of magic objects that I don't know how to create in the fairy tale are also listed. Each chapter also lists other fairy tales that contain references to magical objects of the same nature.

Dinesh Verma

Table of Contents

Ali Baba and Forty Thieves

Ali Baba and the forty thieves is a popular story originally from the Arabian Nights. Ali Baba is a poor woodcutter who accidentally stumbles upon a secret cave where a group of thieves store their treasures. The cave door opens only when the phrase of "Open Sesame" is spoken in front of it, and closes when the phrase "Close Sesame" is invoked. Ali Baba gathers treasures from the cave and brings it home. His greedy, but somewhat dim-witted brother persuades him to give up the secret. However, when the brother enters the cave, he forgets the pass phrase, and is caught and killed by the thieves. Ali Baba brings back the body of his brother, thereby revealing to the thieves that their secret is known to someone else. The thieves use a variety of plots to identify and kill Ali Baba, but his faithful slave Morgiana foils the plots and kills them all using a variety of tricks of her own. As a reward, Morgiana is married to Ali Baba's son and the entire family lives happily ever after.

The story is a clever set of plots and counter-plots between the thieves and Ali Baba (plus Morgiana). However, there is only one magical object in the entire story, namely the cave that opens using the pass phrase of "Open Sesame".

1

Let us see how we can create such a magical cave using modern technology.

To people who are used to systems like Apple's Siri[2], the idea of computers recognizing speech would be relatively passé. In order to create the cave that opens with the magic password, one needs to couple the speech processing technology with the mechanism to operate a door so that it can be opened and closed.

The door operation mechanism is standard fare, e.g. almost every commercial building has doors that can detect the presence of someone in front of the door, and open automatically when someone is in front of the door. It can use either piezoelectric sensors or optical sensors.

Piezeoelectric sensors use elements that change their electric conductivity when compressed, resulting in sensors that can activate a current when someone is standing on a given spot. The optical sensors would detect that someone is present by sending a light beam and see if it is getting blocked.

---

[2] https://www.apple.com/ios/siri/

A rough sketch of the current systems which are present almost ubiquitously is shown below. The sensor detects if a person is present, and sends this signal to the processors. The processor has a simple program which would instruct the actuator to open the door if a person is present, and to close it otherwise. Depending on the actual door mechanism, the actuator will either move apart two panels of a sliding door to open it or move them together to close it, or use a piston to swing the door inside or outside.

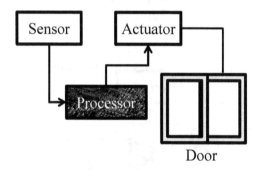

Door

To build the magical cave of the robbers, what we need to do is to replace (or rather augment) the presence sensor with the speech processing component. We can add microphones to the door, and enhance the software on the processor so that it can understand whether the pass phrase has been activated. The presence sensor can be dispensed with but has an important value -- one can only trigger the more complicated speech processing software only when someone is present in front of the door. The software on the processor is more complex now, but the physical arrangement is not that much different from the currently deployed automatically opening doors.

The new setup just consists of additional mircophones that are installed on the door, or in an area near the door where they can pick up the sounds uttered by the person in front of the door, as shown in the figure below.

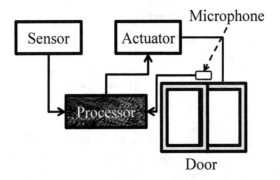

The software on the processor is much more complex now than before. It has to match that the right passphrase is uttered. It can be much simpler than the general purpose speech

4

processing systems like Siri, since all it has to do is to check whether the phrase "Open Sesame" or "Close Sesame" has been spoken.

The interesting part about this magic cave door is that all the components that are required to implement it are readily available. Any enthusiastic DIY person can create such a voice-activated door using components. Speech processing software is available in open domain from various sources, and microphones/systems which allow easy programming are also available. If you are not willing to spend the time integrating open source speech processing packages, you can use the cloud-based services that offer the ability to include speech processing in your application, such as IBM Watson Speech to Text[3] and similar cloud based services. For the sake of demonstration, you can use an old Android or iOS Smartphone to act as the microphone and the processor, and use a Raspberry Pi to control the door actuator. For an extra enhancement, one can camouflage the doors to look like an active cave.

As a matter of fact, modern technology can

---

[3]   https://www.ibm.com/watson/services/speech-to-text/

5

easily make the cave a lot more secure than the thieves had. By adding a camera to the set of sensors that are used, the software on the processor can check the face of the person uttering the pass phrase. Then, the magic cave would only open for the leader of the thieves, and trespassers like Ali Baba would not be able to sneak into the cave. That will save the life of his greedy brother, and not lead Ali Baba or Morgiana into the happy life they lead, so we should all be happy that the thieves did not use the magic of video analysis, and just restricted themselves to speech processing.

There are other magical doors in fantasy and myths that can be realized today using the same approach. Magical doors, which can be opened only by reciting a spell is a staple fare in the fantasy genre. With modern speech processing technologies, these magic spells are nothing but a set of passphrases that need to be matched against to open the door.

As a specific instance, let us consider J.R. Tolkien's fabulously popular novel - *The Lord of the Rings*. As Gandalf and the Fellowship of the Ring undertake their journey to destroy the ring, they encounter the magical doors of Durin which provide entrance to the dwarf mines of Moria. Gandalf spends a significant amount of time deciphering the runes on the door, before realizing that he needs to speak "Friend" and that pass-phrase will open the door. That door will be a straight-forward implementation of the system described in this chapter.

Given that *The Lord of the Rings* was written in the 1940s, we can conclude that speech activated doors would have been considered magical in that decade by a reasonable number of people. The engineers and computer scientists who have made that magical concept become technically viable in less than a century deserve a significant number of accolades.

Bluebeard

Bluebeard is a French tale about a wealthy and powerful nobleman who has married several times, but all his previous wives have mysteriously disappeared. He persuades a poor beautiful girl to be his wife. The wife and Bluebeard live in a great castle with many rooms. When Bluebeard goes away on a trip, he gives his wife the keys to all the rooms but forbids her from entering one special room.

The wife cannot resist temptation and enters the special room. To her horror, she discovers that the room contains the corpses of the previous wives of Bluebeard. Furthermore, the key has turned bloody and the wife is unable to wash the blood off the key despite multiple attempts.

Bluebeard gets notified by magic of the door being opened, and returns home. He prepares to kill his wife who has sent for her brothers for help. She stalls Bluebeard with a set of excuses until her brothers arrive on the scene. They kill Bluebeard and rescue their sister.

The key is the magical object in the story, and has two magical aspects. The first is the fact that it changes color when the room is opened.

8

The second is the fact that Bluebeard learns of the fact that the room has been opened, prompting him to return back.

Like any popular legend, there are various versions of Bluebeard, and in some the key turns blood because it drops into the blood of the previously murdered wives. In other versions, Bluebeard just happens to return back instead of getting a magical notification. Nevertheless, let us consider both magical properties -- Bluebeard has the ability to learn remotely when the chamber was opened, and the key has the magical property that it will turn red when it was used to open the chamber.

If you want to create a secret chamber with the provision that you will be immediately notified if anyone opens it, what you need is a sensor that detects whether the door was opened, and a network that can alert and notify you of the status of the sensor. Thanks to the ubiquity of such sensors, the ubiquity of cellular networks, and the almost universal carriage of cell-phones on our person, the chamber of Bluebeard can be created by anyone at relatively modest cost.

The DIY magician of today needs to get a contact sensor (e.g. one which are used by Home Security Monitoring companies), connect it to a processor (a Raspberry Pi would be more than adequate) to monitor its status, and have

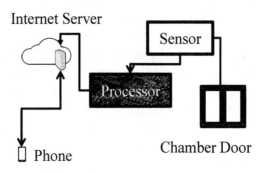

the processor have network connectivity (either WiFi or a cellular card, with the latter being a substantially cheaper approach than the latter for operational costs). The software on the processor can send a text notification to the phone of the person who needs to be notified, or for those who don't mind writing a few more lines of code, use any of the various communication protocols to send a notification to a custom developed application for a Smartphone. My personal preference will be to run a simple server on the Internet to which the sensor sends its status and have the application on the Smartphone poll it periodically to assess

10

the status of the secret chamber, resulting in the system shown above. Other programmers may opt for different design of the setup.

Like the sound activated door of Ali Baba, the chamber that notifies Bluebeard about any trespassing attempt is something any motivated DIYer can assemble today.

The other magical object is the key which would not be washed clean of its blood. The key is essentially an indicator of the fact that it was used to open the door. By default, it is in the off state, changes to the on state when the door is opened, and would remain in the on state till its owner Bluebeard resets it. The indicator should be inside the key, since anything on the outside can be washed away.

There are many ways to make such an indicator, and here is a simple design. Let the surface of the key be made up partially from semi-transparent material, e.g. a small strip of see-through clear plastic. The hollow inside of the key contains a small red LED bulb, and a small battery. The battery by default is in a position where it won't be connected to the LED. However, when the key in inserted into the door and turned, a mechanism closes the connection and the red LED turns on, giving the

11

key the impression of being bloody as the red light shows through the semi-transparent part of the key.

One possible way to close the connection would be to have a permanent magnet inside the door lock, and an iron plate inside the key. When the key is turned and opens the door, the magnet pulls the plate into a location where the circuit is closed. A mechanical lock can prevent the iron plate from going back into the original

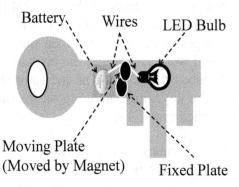

Battery Wires LED Bulb

Moving Plate
(Moved by Magnet) Fixed Plate

position.

The setup is as shown in the rough sketch above which shows the configuration of the internal system when the electric circuit is closed. Since the setup is battery powered, it can also include a small processor to send an alert to the owner that the key has been used.

There are other designs for an indicator key which do not require a battery. After all, batteries do have their own issues. They have a finite life-time, and would need to be replaced, which requires a way to open the key. While that can be achieved by having the key outside consist of two interlocking parts which are connected by a cleverly concealed screw, some people may prefer a battery-free indicator key.

One possible battery-free indicator key can be built by using a small bag of red dye inside a hollow see-through key. The key could have a small hole through which a needle can puncture the dye-bag, releasing the red dye inside the

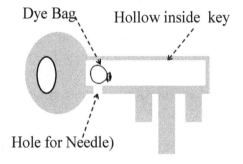

Dye Bag   Hollow inside key

Hole for Needle)

key. The needle to puncture the hole can be the part of the lock mechanism in the door. As the key turns in the door, the internal bolts of the lock push the needle through the hole in the key to puncture the dye-bag.

When the dye bag would be punctured, some of the dye would leak outside thorugh the puncture hole, staining the outside of the key. The bulk of the dye would be inside the hollow part of the key, resulting in a bloody key that can not be washed clean.

The legend of Bluebeard is from an era where batteries and the Internet did not exist. However, a smart locksmith could have easily created a hollow key with a dye-bag inside. While Bluebeard would not have gotten a notification (let us assume he just happened to return back suddenly by chance), he would know from the stained key that the secret room had been opened. The legend as narrated might have actually happened. Apart from the magic key whose blood could not be washed off, all other parts of the story are quite believable.

If you do end up making the magic key of Bluebeard, just do the world a favor and use it for good instead of evil.

Other fairy tales

There are other fairy tales that use a magical object which is very similar to the magic key. In the German fairy tale of *The Fitcher Bird*, the devil marries three sisters in turn, handling them each an egg and prohibiting them from entering a room. When they enter the forbidden room, the egg drops and they cannot wash the blood off it. The youngest daughter leaves the egg outside, and the devil does not realize that she has opened the room.

In the Italian fairy tale version of the same, entitled *How the Devil Married Three Sisters,* the object is a flower which is singed when the forbidden door is opened. The forbidden room contains fire from hell, instead of the blood from the murdered bodies.

The magic egg could be made in the same way as the magic key, except in a different shape. The dye bag needs to be punctured by means of the force when the egg falls on the ground, or equivalently the LED can be powered on when the force triggers a circuit.

In the Italian version, the flower is triggered to take on a singed appearance because of the fire. In this case, one probably does not even need any magic, since a normal flower will be singed by a normal fire. Of course, one can also create an electronic flower which changes its color when it is exposed to heat from a fire.

15

Snow White

The story of Snow White is well known. She was a pretty princess whose vain step-mother was jealous of her beauty. The step-mother had a mirror to which she posed the question regularly -- "Mirror, Mirror on the Wall, who is the fairest of them all?" The mirror would respond back with the name and image of the person who was the fairest among all the people in the Kingdom.

Apart from the magic mirror, majority of Snow White story is a believable story of human emotions, including envy, cruelty and kindness. The mirror would usually name the step-mother as the fairest maiden, until Snow White grows up and she becomes the fairest one. The jealous step-mother orders her to be killed, but the huntsman ordered to do so listens to his conscience and lets Snow White go. She finds refuge with seven brothers who are somewhat short. Of course, the mirror maintains the answer that Snow White is the fairest in the land, revealing her existence to the step-mother.

The evil step-mother tries different tricks to kill Snow White, but does not succeed. A poison causes Snow White to go into coma from which she awakes when a prince kisses her, and she

16

lives happily ever after with the prince.

Let us see how we can recreate Queen's magic mirror. With the wonders of modern processors, smart algorithms, ubiquitous cameras and the universal connectivity of the Internet, the magic mirror can indeed be realized today.

To create the magic mirror, take a large display screen, the same screen that is used in televisions, which is in the shape and size of a full-length mirror. On the periphery of the display screen, attach an array of microphones, speakers and cameras. The cameras would capture the image of the person standing in front of the mirror, while the microphone and speakers would let the magic mirror interact with the person in front and hold a conversation.

The entire assembly would be driven by a computer in the background. The computer would need to have a database of all the maidens in the land, and would run the software comparing their fairness. We will come to the question of how that database will be created and maintained shortly. For the moment, let us just assume that the database exists and is up to date.

Creating a physical system that comprises all of those components together is something that can be easily done today. There will be some interesting design and engineering questions to

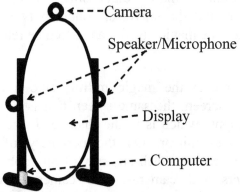

be answered, such as the number and position of the microphones, speakers and cameras respectively, the shape of the display, where the power supply cord should be located to not be visible, the location and positioning of the computer, the size of the disk that maintains the database of fair maidens, etc. Those questions can be answered in a variety of ways, mostly on the personal preference of the designer. We are ignoring all cost concerns, but at the current prices of electronics, the bill is likely to be no more than the price of a high-end television set.

The real magic would lie not in the physical setup, but in the software that one would run on the computer. The software would have multiple components. The first component would be a speech processing system which would take the sounds from the microphones and translate them into the question being asked by the speaker. Instead of the user alerting the system by using a standard introductory phrase like "Alexa" or "Hello Google", the system can use an introductory phrase of "Mirror, Mirror on the Wall". After that, the exact speech can be translated into the question, which for the sake of fairy tale will be "Who is the fairest of them all?".

Assuming that the database of all the people in the land is available, the software needs to assign a metric of fairness to each person, and select the highest metric among them. The metric of fairness can be defined in a variety of ways. If fairness refers to the color of the face, a color comparison can be used -- although one could argue that fairness should refer to a measure of beauty rather than to just the color of the face. Other metrics of fairness or beauty may be defined, which include measurement of facial symmetry, or relative ratio of facial features which could provide alternative measure of fairness. Some researchers have tried to create mathematical and computational measures of beauty[4]. The person developing the software can choose the appropriate definition of fairness among them. Similarly, the software may decide to filter some type of people from the database, e.g. only select fairness for women and exclude men, or vice-versa depending on what the preferences of the owner of the magic mirror is.

The difficult part in creating the magic mirror would be in compiling a current database of all the people in the land. Here, the ubiquitous presence of video cameras used for surveillance can come in quite handy. The cameras can collect the images of all the people who are in the land (depending on how land is defined), collect information about the person identified in the image (e.g. by crawling through the set of linked friends on social media, use the metadata available on images on the Internet etc.) and thus compile a database of different people on the land. The database of images would allow the identification of the fairest person, even if the metadata about who the person is may not

[4] Gunes, Hatice, and Massimo Piccardi. "Assessing facial beauty through proportion analysis by image processing and supervised learning." International journal of human-computer studies 64.12 (2006): 1184-1199.

always be available.

If one defines the database to be a little less general, e.g. only selecting people who are part of the social network of the person owning the magic mirror, the database can be updated using the social media links. Assuming the owner signs in with their favorite social network account[5], the database building software can crawl through the set of all pictures belonging to the friends in the network. It can then use the annotations/metadata available for each picture to make a database of friends, along with their latest profile picture. This database can then be used to find the fairest one in the social network.

In conclusion, if you are a bit handy with cobbling together sensors and devices, and reasonably handy with programming, you can easily create a magic mirror using data available on the Internet and commercially available technology.

---

[5] Any social network that contains pictures of participants (e.g. facebook, linkedin etc.) can be used for this purpose. Note that the book is not endorsing any specific social network, and is not endorsed by any social network.

The Legend of Patna

Patna is an ancient city and the capital of the state of Bihar in India. Its old name is Pataliputra, named after the couple who founded the city, Queen Patali and King Putrak. The legend about the establishment of the city involves three magical objects that are also mentioned in several other legends and fairy tales.

Putrak was an industrious young man, who left his home due to the bad behavior of his father and uncles. During his travels, he came across two giants fighting over the possession of three magical objects. The first object was a magic pot that would provide any dish the user asked for. The second object was a pair of shoes that would let the wearer fly in the air. The third object was a stick and any house or building drawn on the ground with that stick would be created in reality.

Putrak tricked the demons into giving him the three magical objects. Using these objects, he charmed and married the beautiful Princess Patali. Patali's father was opposed to the marriage, so the young couple absconded using the magic shoes, stopping at the bank of Ganges River where the current city of Patna is located.

Putrak drew the plan of a city using his stick which became real in almost no time. Putrak named this magically created city after his wife and himself, with the wife's name coming first as it is traditional in India (and the final k getting dropped over time).

Let us consider the magic objects one by one, and discuss how we can create them today.

The Magic Stick

Anything that is drawn by the magic stick gets recreated rapidly. How can we create similar capability rapidly today?

Let us consider any drawing that is made by the stick. We can take a picture of that drawing with a camera and convert it into a digital blueprint of a building (or sets of buildings that need to be drawn). A software program on a computer can further interpret and enhance the image to a plan for the building, e.g. translate the image into the number of floors in the building, or the nature of the building, and provide any missing details from a set of pre-existing templates. Armed with this digital description of the building/buildings, we need to rapidly create them for real.

For a simple building without a lot of

23

fixtures, e.g. a warehouse, large 3D-printers can create houses very rapidly. Such machines, which effectively pour concrete that sets in a new pattern, have been demonstrated[6]. Similarly, structures with bricks can be laid by machines controlled with computers[7].

With the help of modern robots, such automation need not be limited to simply bricks and poured concrete. Assuming there is a supply of building materials; one can make robots that perform the different tasks needed to build a house.

When a house is built, the builders follow a prescribed set of procedures. First the concrete is poured to make the foundation. Then the base of the house is laid. This is followed by putting in the various studs that will support the walls. The basic frame of the house is put on top of that. The inner electric wiring and the plumbing is established. The septic tank or connection to the sewer line is installed. By following a very well defined sequence of steps, a house is constructed.

----

[6]http://www.businessinsider.com/3d-printer-builds-house-in-24-hours-2014-1
    [7]http://inhabitat.com/incredible-bricklaying-robot-can-build-a-house-in-just-two-days/

There is nothing in this set of instructions that a robot, equipped with a camera, the ability to move, and the right appendage to perform the required task (nailing, hammering, etc.) cannot perform. Since the building of the house is a routine process which requires following a specific sequence of well-defined processes, such robots can create houses much faster than a team of humans can. Furthermore, they are less likely to make a mistake during the construction process.

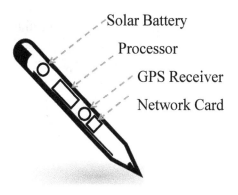

Solar Battery

Processor

GPS Receiver

Network Card

The magic stick of legend is a highly portable device which is carried on the person of the hero. All the different robots needed to make a building or a set of buildings cannot be carried on the person of an individual. However, thanks to the marvel of modern technology, that problem can be easily solved. We can consider the magic stick as a single user interface device. The stick would embed within itself a small processor which includes a GPS location system, as well as a network card to communicate with a remote system with robots that can build the building. To power the device, let us add a solar battery to the mix as well. The resulting stick, shown schematically above, would be something portable that can be carried on someone's person easily.

Complementing this stick would be the real system which is capable of making the building come to reality. One instantiation of this system would be a depot which contains a store of building material, the stock of robots of various types that can construct the building from the materials, and one or two self-driving trucks which can ferry the material and robots to any location.

When the user draws the building or buildings on the ground with the stick, the location is recorded, and a message sent to the depot. The depot dispatches a self-driving truck with building material and robots to the right location. The first robot on the ground can take a digital image of the structures drawn on the ground, convert that to a digital format, and then instructs the remaining robots to do the required construction as discussed above.

So, the magic stick which helps in creating a building or an entire city by drawing it on paper is very much attainable today. Whether it will actually be realized as a common practice is open to question -- since it depends on factors beyond technical feasibility, such as the impact on jobs of workers, the reaction of the labor unions, and the cost effectiveness of a robotic solution for house construction.

There is a major difference between the magic stick in the legend and the magic stick as we have described today. In legends, all the material required to build the houses appears out of thin air, and the hero does not have to pay for it. In real-life, the supplies for the buildings need to be paid for and obtained from some supplier of the same. However, under the constraint that we can not violate the law on conservation of mass, this is a fairly good approximation of the magic staff. [8]

---

[8] Some people may want to point out that energy can be converted into mass, and so theoretically one can

27

Magic Shoes

Magic shoes occur in not just the legend of Patna, but in many other fairy tales throughout the world. It would be interesting to explore how such shoes may be developed in practice.

The technology that comes closest to the magic shoes is that of personal one man helicopters, personal flying cars and personal jetpacks. Several companies have tried to bring out such products, although unfortunately none of them seems to have a commercial success with their products yet. Some examples include the Gen H-4 kit from Japanese Gen Corporation[9], and the Martin Corporation personal Jetpack[10]. In essence, these are small cars/helicopters that use a set of propellers powered by a compact gasoline fueled engines and they generate enough up-thrust to lift a person in the air. Add in a few controls for directing motion, and you can create a flying car/one man helicopter or a jet-pack. Several

---

create the building materials out of thin air. However, with the current state of technology, that remains out of human reach for practical home building. The system that is described in this chapter is within the feasibility of modern technology.

[9] http://en.gen-corp.jp/
[10] http://www.martinjetpack.com/

28

prototypes have already been built and demonstrated, and some of them are available commercially. The price which will run into several tens of thousand dollars is a bit daunting, but someone with sufficiently deep pockets can afford such devices today.

The one place where the same technology has become commercially viable is that of drones. Small drones, usually consisting of four small propellers, can be bought for a couple of hundred dollars, can carry light loads such as a mounted camera, and can be controlled via a remote on the ground.

The flying cars and jetpacks of today are massive machines into which a person climbs. It will be a stretch of imagination to call them any type of shoes, but they do demonstrate that it is possible to create small propellers that have enough up-thrust to support the weight of a person and keep them in the air for a couple of hours.

Another relevant technology is that of magnetic levitation. It has been used successfully for trains, display cases, some specialized industrial manufacturing processes, and by street conjurers. If you walk around in touristy areas of London, UK, you are likely to see a few street artists standing on platforms levitating in air.

Magnetic levitation works by having two pieces of magnets that repel each other because they have the same magnetic pole facing each other. One of the magnets is a temporary one, e.g. generated by means of an electric current. One of them is affixed to the ground, and the other is levitating platform. The amount of weight they can support depends on the strength of the magnetic field. And having such magnets lift up the weight of a normal human being is well within the realm of current engineering as a proven technology.

Unfortunately, magnetic levitation does not come close to the capabilities of magic shoes either. It can lift a person in the air on selected spots (e.g. where one can affirm one of the two required magnets on the ground). However, stepping outside the magnetic field would have the wearer crashing to the ground very rapidly.

Having looked at the set of relevant technologies, let us consider what will be the minimum requirements to create a pair of magic shoes. To come close to satisfy the objectives of the fairy tales, they must (at a minimum):

- Be something that a person can step into.
- Be able to lift a person in the air
- Be able to move horizontally when the person is in the air

As an example of the first condition, we will stretch the definition of shows to include long ice skis like shapes. There are a few technical challenges that need to be overcome to make the shoes fly. They mechanism within the shoes need to generate enough up-thrust in the air so that they can lift a typical grown-up person and the mechanism. The person needs to be able to be in a stable position as he or she flies through the air, and the flight path must be controllable. Furthermore, from the feats attained by the wearer of the shoes in the legends, the shoes enable an almost vertical take-off and landing since the hero wearing the shoes usually lands on a high tower when the pretty princess is waiting for him.

Let us use the strategy that we will use two drones or UAVs as our shoes. Imagine a person strapping on a pair of UAVs and using them to fly. If there is enough lift in the UAVs, the person can be lifted up in the air, and if the two UAVs could be controlled in close coordination, the person can move back and forth in the air.

31

The initial setup will be like in the diagram below.

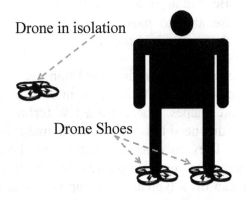

There are many issues with this initial setup of using drones as shoes. First, the currently available commercial drones are not powerful enough to lift a human being. Assuming that we can create a drone with the required amount of uplift, the shoes will leave the person in a very precarious situation and balancing the drones will be a big challenge. And furthermore, how will the person control the drone back and forth.

As the jetpacks and personal helicopters show, we can create commercial propellers and drones that generate sufficient up-thrust to hold up a person. However, these propellers are very large. The typical jetpack capable of lifting a man would have a propeller 2 to 3 ft long.

Instead of a shoe, let us use a ski like structure that has two propellers, i.e. a system that is 5-7 ft long, and has a propeller at the front and back. Let us connect the two skis for each foot with cross connects that are now maintained in a fixed position. The setup now looks like the rough sketch below.

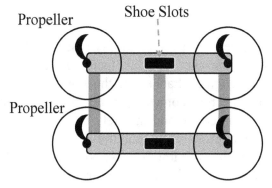

Propeller

Shoe Slots

Propeller

The cross connects and the ski does make it a rather clumsy shoe, but it is something that one can step into. The next hurdle is figuring out how to keep this configuration stable as the contraption flies in the air with a person standing in the shoe slots.

The stabilization can be done if we add a processor to the entire system to control the speed of each propeller. The processor runs the software that maintains the speed of each

33

propeller to create an up-thrust that can maintain the ski in a stable horizontal position. That type of software is what has allowed commercial drones to stabilize their propellers and make them easy to fly. The same software and setup can be used to stabilize the contraption we are making. Usually, the stabilization requires the inclusion of a gyroscope that can be programmed for optimal maintenance of the orientation.

We need a power supply that will be adequate for the task at hand. A gasoline powered engine attached at the bottom of the skis or the cross-connect can do that task. We would also need to add in safety mechanisms to reduce the probability that the flier would be hurt. At the minimum, this should include covering the propeller appropriately so the person does not accidentally step into them.

The only thing remaining to be done is to provide a control for the system to navigate it and an application on a Smartphone provides the right mechanism to do so.

The above structure will likely be deemed illegal to fly in every nation. Furthermore, a lot of hard engineering and careful programming needs to be put to make the entire system work as desired. However, the intention is to show that something that can be called (with some poetic license) a shoe can be created with current technology.

As the technology for creating up-thrust improves, (e.g. we use jets instead of propellers) or powerful higher rotation propellers are attained, the size of the ski poles can be reduced so that the system looks more and more like a shoe.

While the magic shoes are technically feasible, building them requires some sophisticated mechanical engineering and equally complex programming. This is definitely not a DIY task for a casual tinkerer.

Magic Pot

The magic pot is a device which will provide you with any dish that you ask it for. Place the magic pot on a table, utter a chant like "Magic Pot, give me a grilled cheese sandwich," or any other dish, and shortly thereafter, you will have that desired dish in the pot.

To make the magic pot, we will attach a processor to the pot, which has a network card connected to a wide area network (e.g. the cellular network), and software capable of voice recognition. With the voice recognition, the magic pot can understand what dish is being requested.

The challenge remains of getting the desired dish into the magic pot. Since we don't have the technology to teleport food (or any object) yet, we will resort to a small stratagem to make the magic pot real. The magic pot will work only when it is placed under the open sky.

The equipment on the magic pot will also include a GPS based position locator. When the wish for the dish will be made, the location and the desired dish will be relayed to a commercial kitchen. The kitchen will prepare the dish, just like we place take-out orders to any restaurant over the phone today.

Once the dish is prepared, it is placed in a pot identical to the magic pot used to place the order. A drone that takes this dish, flies to the location of the magic pot, places the new pot and takes the old pot away. As it swaps the pots out, it can also reconfigure the ownership of the pots.

In an alternative approach, the drone could carry the dish in a container and empty the container into the magic pot. This approach does not require swapping pots, just that the drone contain a mechanism by which the contents of the container can be transferred to the pot. For liquid or semi-liquid dishes, this transfer can be done by tilting the container to pour the dish into the pot. Solid dishes which are plated (e.g. a piece of salmon with a salad on the side), can be transferred in the following manner. The dish is plated properly on a disposable (e.g. paper or plastic) plate before it is put on the drone. When the drone reaches the pot, it transfers the plate to the dish by means of retractable claws that place the plate gingerly on the pot. The drone would also need to fly with care – so that the plated dish is not disturbed.

The weight of the dish supplied in this manner will be limited, and the drone flight can only be operated if legally allowed in the area. Nevertheless, this will come fairly close to the concept of the magic pot in fairy tales.

The only difference, like that of the magic stick, is that someone needs to pay for the dish that is prepared and delivered to the person who made the wish.

Prince of Vardhaman

Vardhaman is a city in the state of West Bengal in India. As per legend, a prince of the city left to search for a lost jeweled arrow. During the search, he came across the land of a wizard, meeting his daughter at the outskirts of the city. The prince and wizard's daughter fall in love, but her father disapproves of their marriage.

The father puts in hard tasks to the prince which includes identifying the princess from her other identical looking and dressed sisters, sow a thousand pounds of sesame seeds in a single day, and recollect all the seeds on the next day from the ground. The wizard's daughter helps him in all the tasks. For the first, she wears the necklace on her head to stand out from the other sisters. For the second, she lets the prince sleep while her magical ox sows the seeds by itself. For the third, she sends in a swarm of ants to collect the seeds back.

Annoyed at his failure to kill the prince, the wizard sends the prince to relay a message to his evil brother, who would catch and kill the prince as soon as the message is delivered. The wizard's daughter provides the prince with a bowl of dust, a vase of water, a bundle of thorns and a brazier with burning charcoals, with instructions on when to throw these on the ground when the evil brother is about to catch him. The prince shouts the message to the wizard's brother from a distance and rides away immediately. When the wizard's brother gives chase, he throws each of the objects in turn. The bowl of dust turns into a mountain, the vase of water turns into a river, the thorns turn into a thick forest, and the charcoal turns into a blazing fire. Each of these objects block the evil brother, and the prince returns safely.

When the prince returns, the wizard's daughter elopes with him to return to Vardhaman. When the wizard tries to catch them, she tricks him with some smart disguises and clever talk. The confused wizard is unable to catch them and the happy couple reaches Vardhaman to live happily ever after.

Ignoring the clever tricks of the princess, the legend introduces six magical objects. The first magical object is the ox which sows thousand pounds of sesame seeds in a day. The second are the magical ants which collect back all the seeds in a day. The other four are the bowl of dust, a vase of water, a bundle of thorns and a brazier with burning charcoals, each turning into a large barrier to save the prince from his pursuer. Let us examine how these magical objects can be created today.

Magic Ox

The magic ox is a beast that could sow a huge quantity of sesame seeds in a single day. While a thousand pounds of sesame seeds may be impossible for a single individual to sow within a day, it would be within a reasonable capacity of a mechanized agricultural machine. So, if we consider the magic ox as simply a mechanical planter, then it would be perfectly within the capacity of a machine to handle this amount of seeds. As a reference point, the John Deere DB120[11] planter can operate with 4 tons of seed, which is 8 times the amount the prince was asked to handle.

The one modern enhancement that needs to be done to the mechanical planter is to convert it from a device operated by a human being to something that runs on its own. Thanks to the advances in technology for self-driving cars, combining that with a mechanical planter will be considered a simple engineering exercise today.

---

[11] https://en.wikipedia.org/wiki/John_Deere_DB120

So, if the wizard's daughter had a self-driving mechanical planter (with possibly a self-driving mechanical tiller to plough the land before planting the seeds), she can accomplish the task at hand in a few hours, spending the rest of the time having fun with the prince.

Magic Ants

The magic ants had a different task to perform, namely collect all the seeds that were in the field and return them to the bushels. This task too, thanks to the marvels in robotic technology and the Internet of Things, is quite doable today.

Each magic ant would be a small robot with a processor, a camera, appendages to grab the seeds, an ability to move, and a source of power. The power could be solar. The processors could be fairly small, but still be powerful. As an example, the Micro Mote being developed at University of Michigan is smaller than the size of a U.S. nickel.[12] The small size does not prevent the computer from being capable enough, and it would still be more powerful

---

[12] Y. Lee, et. al, "A modular 1mm3 die-stacked sensing platform with optical communication and multi-modal energy harvesting,". In International Solid-State Circuits Conference, Feb. 2012.

than the computer that landed the first mission on the moon.

With such computing capacity at hand, a large swarm of such mechanical ants can be programmed to search for sesame seeds and bring them back to a collection spot. The tiny camera in the mechanical ants can recognize the seeds, they can dig for a specific distance to find the seeds, and carry them back. A large enough swarm of mechanical ants can perform the task within a few hours. All that the princess has to do is to command the swarm of ants with a central computer, and spend time with the prince while the ants do all the work.

Magical Path Blockers

The four remaining magical objects are path blockers for the pursuing evil magician. As each of these objects in thrown on the ground, it becomes a huge natural structure that blocks the pursuer.

While the law of conversation of mass prevents any small object to suddenly become a huge object of its own, an object can be used to throw obstructions in the path of a pursuer under two conditions (i) that the right mechanism for blocking the path be prepared in advance and (ii) that the object be used as a trigger to activate the mechanism that is prepared in advance.

For the bowl of dust that becomes a mountain, let us assume that a mechanism to release a large number of boulders, stones and dust is prepared in advance. If the path of pursuit goes between a pair of hills, the sides of the hills may be implanted with dynamite sticks which will cause the side of the hill to be blown away and fill the intervening path with debris. In that case, the bowl of dust thrown on the ground simply acts as the triggering mechanism

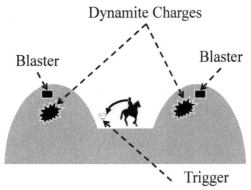

for the dynamite to be exploded.

The triggering mechanism which will be activated when it falls on the ground can be created using a piezoelectric switch. When piezoelectric materials are subject to pressure, their electric conductivity changes and they can pass electricity through. This can activate a small processor to send a remote signal to the mechanism that controls the dynamite. The rough sketch of the system is shown in the figure above this paragraph.

Instead of a dynamite charge blasting the rocks, the preset mechanism could also be holding back a set of boulders or rocks maintained on the hilly areas by a gate which is opened by the trigger to unleash an avalanche of stones.

The other three magic objects blocking the path would work in the same manner. If there are tanks of water on the hillside, then opening the tank gates could cause a temporary flooding of the region between the hills. That would be the mechanism used with the magic jar of water.

The magic bundle of thorns would be a similar trigger except that it would unleash a set of logs and other vegetation matter that would fall down the hills. The vegetation matter can also contain several thorns or other sharp objects that could be used to block the path.

The fire itself would not require that the mechanism be used on a hillside, but if the path went through a series of flammable materials, e.g. dried grass and other types of dry plants, a forest fire could be triggered by the brazier of burning coals.

With proper preparation, the wizard's daughter could save the prince by instructing him to throw the right trigger at the right location once he has cleared the dangerous area.

Other Fairy Tales

There are many other fairy tales which follow a theme similar to the Prince of Vardhaman. The typical plot consists of the hero falling in love with the heroine, and is given difficult tasks to perform by an evil protector of the heroine. The magic objects or magic skill of the heroine lets the hero perform the tasks easily. Finally, the hero and the heroine escape with the help of the magic objects, which allow them to put in road-blocks in the way of a pursuing protector.

Fairy tales that include the motif of magic objects hampering an enemy in pursuit include *Master Maid* (a Norwegian fairy tale), *Water Nixie* (a German fairy tale from) and *Nix Nought Nothing* (an English fairy tale) which is a retelling of the Scottish fairy tale of *Nicht Nought Nothing*. The preplanned escape system can explain the magical escape in all of these stories, although the exact description of the magical object tends to be a bit different in each of these stories.

There are other fairy tales in which the hero and heroine thwart pursuers by changing shapes. Unfortunately, modern technology has not yet created an obvious way for a man to change into a church or a pigeon, so those tales will have to remain magical for now.

There are several fairy tales which require the hero to do work that is beyond human capability, and is performed by means of magical animals or other type of magic by the heroine. Work that would be considered difficult by old standards of doing things manually, can be performed relatively easily using robots, mechanical devices and other types of automation that we take for granted today. Some examples of these tales are *The Two King's Children* (a German fairy tale), *Master Maid*, as well as several stories related to spinning large amounts of yarn (see *The Three Spinners* chapter in the book).

Beauty and the Beast

Beauty and the Beast is a famous French fairy tale which has been made even more popular by its rendition into films. The story has a beautiful girl who agrees to spend time as a willing captive of a ferocious beast in exchange for her father. The castle of the beast is enchanted with talking candles, pots, pans and other household items. Beauty uses a magic mirror to see her father who is sick and asks the Beast permission to go to see her father. When she returns, the beast is dying. Beauty professes her love for the beast who is transformed into a handsome prince as her enchantment which made him a beast is broken.

The story has many magical objects, the enchanted household items that talk, and the magic mirror being the most prominent ones. Let us consider the various enchanted objects that can talk, and see how those could be created.

Talking Objects

In the popular pictures associated in the *story of Beauty and the Beast*, the castle of the Beast is filled with enchanted objects, a talking teacup and tea-pot, candle-stands that can talk and light by themselves, furniture that can talk and adjust

47

their position etc. The nice part of living at the current time is that all of these talking objects can be made real, although they may turn out to be a bit expensive.

Let us consider the basic task of a talking teacup and a talking tea-pot. For the basic function of talking, one can take a system consisting of a pair of microphones/speakers and a processor. Each of these can be made reasonably small so that you can imagine them put together on a rectangular strip which is less that a centimeter on both sides. On a larger object, larger form factors for speakers can be used. The larger the speaker, the better quality of sound can be generated. Such a strip would be just placed on the surface of the magic object. The power for these components can come from a solar battery that is also embedded within the strip.

The processor would need to implement the software for voice recognition and natural speech synthesis, same as what systems like IBM Watson Speech processing engine[13], or Apple's Siri[14] do. Instead of the current

---

[13]https://www.ibm.com/watson/services/speech-to-text/

[14] https://www.apple.com/ios/siri/

implementation of these systems which run off a cloud-hosted service, that software needs to be run on the processor in the object.

At this point, a hardware engineer may object that the processor that can be built in this manner won't have the computation capacity to run the complex processes of speech understanding and response creation that is implemented by systems in the cloud. If one were to create a processor with that much capability, they would not be the small tiny ones that can fit into a small strip form factor.

The criticism is valid, even though we can envision a very near-term future where even tiny processors are able to perform tasks of comparable complexity. After all, the weakest mobile phone we carry in our pocket today has more computation power than the computers that landed man on the moon a few decades ago. Nevertheless, let us consider how we would deal with the situation when the processor available on the object is not powerful enough.

One way to deal with the limited processing capability in the processor of the strip will be to include a network interface, e.g. a wi-fi interface on the strip as well. The commands can be sent via the wi-fi network to a single server in the house. The server can then perform the required processing for understanding the sounds that a user is making, convert them into natural language, and then respond back to the user with the reply using synthesized voice.

The strip can also include other miniature sensors, e.g. a heat or temperature sensor. When the temperature sensor notices that the liquid in the cup is above some threshold, it can generate synthetic sounds like "ooh! this is hot", or when it falls below a threshold --"The tea is getting cold".

This server inside the castle can control the interactions of all the talking objects within the castle. There could be a multitude of talking pots, talking plates, talking cups, talking candelabras, talking chairs etc, which can be put into the castle, and controlled by the server.

In addition to sending the current state (e.g. temperature), the strip may also contain actuators that can change the state of an object, e.g. turn a candle on or off. These switches can also be created and embedded at a suitable location inside the object.

Magic Mirror
The magic mirror allows Beauty to see the

status of her father when she is away in the Beast's castle. Similarly, it allows her to see the status of the Beast when she is at her father's place, and she returns because the Beast is sick and close to dying.

This magic mirror is available readily in the market today as video cameras used for surveillance. Security personnel in many cities monitor the roads and public transportation locations such as train stations, airports and bus terminals using such video cameras. The feed from the cameras is usually sent to an observation center where several consoles display the video being recorded by the cameras.

A similar magic mirror is available for people to use for video-calls on most popular types of phones. These applications for video-chatting allow anyone to not just see, but also to talk to a friend regardless of distance.

Given that these systems are so ubiquitous, the only effort required to create a magic mirror is to take the display of a Smartphone and wrap it in an enclosure that makes it look like a mirror. You can then connect it to one or more cameras to see what the remote location looks like.

The magic mirror can be created today without any difficulties.

Still Magical

If we can create all the magical talking objects and the magical mirror, we can pretty much recreate the enchanted castle of the Beast without too much difficulty.

However, there are two magical things that we don't know how to create yet with the current state of the technology. The first magic is that of transformation of a handsome prince into a beast and vice-versa the beast regaining his shape once the spell is broken. Changing physical shapes is not yet possible with current technology.

The other magical object that appears in some variations of *Beauty and the Beast* is a magic wishing ring. The wishing ring transports Beauty instantly from the Beast's castle to her father's house. When Beauty wants to return to the castle, she uses the wishing ring again to return in an instant.

That type of teleportation is not yet possible with current state of the technology. Although there have been some advances made in teleportation of small tiny photons using the concept of quantum entanglement, the teleportation of anything of modest size remains beyond the reach of current technology.

Future technological advances may make the magic ring and the transformation of the beast become a reality as well. For the moment though, we can leave those parts as the magical components of the fairy tale.

The Everlasting Pot

In the epic of *Mahabharata*, which narrates the story of a civil war in ancient India, there are many tales that deal with magical objects. One of them includes an *akshay-patra* or the everlasting pot.

The heroine of the epic, the princess of Punjab, is alone in her house one day when she receives some unexpected guests -- a group of hermits who are very hungry after a long journey. They request food and go to wash themselves in a nearby river before eating the meals. To make matters worse, the leader of the group is a hermit known for his bad temper and propensity to curse people at the smallest provocation. Poor princess is ill-prepared and all she can manage to cook is a small pot of rice gruel, barely enough to serve one person. She asks for help from Krishna, who uses his magic to make that small pot of gruel serves every hermit. As soon as the princess serves gruel to one hermit, the pot fills up automatically again with the gruel that can serve the next hermit. Krishna saves the day and prevents the princess from being cursed.

A similar legend of an everlasting pot is associated with Krishna in Eastern India. A poor

54

kid lives on the edge of the forest and needs to go to school to his teacher on the other end of the forest all alone since his single mother has to work and cannot afford to walk with him. The kid is afraid to cross the forest, but her mother pushes him forward and telling him to rely on Krishna to get him across. The kid calls on Krishna to accompany him through the forest. He is answered by a young boy his own age who walks with him across the forest every day.

One day, the school teacher organizes a pot-luck party asking everyone to bring a dish. The poor mother sends the kid empty-handed since she can't afford anything. The kid asks his walking buddy Krishna for help, and Krishna provides him with a small pot of curd, barely enough for one person. The teacher is not too pleased with the small bowl, and pours out a little bit of curd for each kid. However, to his surprise, the pot keeps on refilling with curd till all the kids at school had their fill of the most exquisite curd they ever tasted.

Let us examine how we can make an everlasting pot today. We will define the everlasting pot as a small pot which is full of a meal. Let us (at least in the beginning) assume that the meal is a liquid (curd, gruel, porridge, fish curry etc.). As soon as the liquid is taken out of the pot, it refills again. With this definition, it is very feasible to create such an everlasting pot today. A simple way to create a pot is illustrated in the figure below.

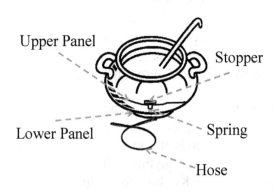

Upper Panel — Stopper — Lower Panel — Spring — Hose

Since we lack the technology to teleport matter at the current time, the everlasting pot needs to be connected to a larger vessel which contains the required amount of meal to serve the large number of guests. The supply of the food from the larger vessel will refill the small pot as soon as it is emptied.

The everlasting pot would need two mechanisms – a mechanism that allows the food in the larger vessel to refill the pot once it is empty and a mechanism that will stop the food from the larger vessel coming into the pot when it is full.

For a liquid meal, an easy way to have the larger vessel fill the pot will be to place the larger vessel at a higher altitude than the everlasting pot. This would allow the liquid to flow into the everlasting pot due to gravity. Suppose a hose connects the everlasting pot to the larger vessel. The everlasting pot could be created with two bottom panels, with a hole in the top panel that is plugged with a stopper with a spring.

When the pot is full, the stopper is weighed down by the weight of the meal, which pushes the spring down. This will close the hole, and no more food will flow into the pot. When the pot is empty, the spring pushes the stopper up allowing the liquid from the larger vessel to flow into the pot.

The pot need not be completely empty before it starts to refill. When the weight of the meal is sufficient to push down on the spring, the pot will not take any food since the hole will be closed. When enough food is removed so that the spring can push upward and open the hole, the pot will start to refill.

This purely mechanical system would give the illusion that the small pot fills up as soon as the liquid from the pot is removed.

The configuration of the pot, when it is full and when it is empty is shown in the figure below.

Empty Pot   Full Pot

The everlasting pot described above is not very portable. It has to stay in one place since it is connected to a hose. If the hose is long and flexible, limited movement may be possible. Furthermore, if the hose is carefully hidden or camouflaged, the system would appear to be very much like the magical pot that fills itself.

Let us consider how we can extend the concept to solid food. Example of solid food which can be put into a pot includes items like fries, hash-browns, or meatballs – stuff that can be served from a pot and does not require exquisite plating. When the food is solid, we cannot rely on the power of gravity to refill the

58

pot. However, we can have a motorized system with a mechanism which would suck in the solid food from a master supply when the everlasting pot in empty. The pot would need a power supply, a sensing mechanism to determine whether the pot is empty or full, and a suction system (like that used in vacuum cleaners) which can suck the food from the master supply when the sensor sees the pot as empty.

This pot will be a bit larger and relatively clumsy due to the need for larger components, but can be designed and implemented with modern technology.

Whether the everlasting pot as described above is useful or commercially viable is debatable. However, it does show that something that comes close enough to an everlasting pot can be created without requiring divine intervention.

Master Maid

The *Master Maid* is a Norwegian fairy tale in which a prince is hired by a giant. In his castle, the prince finds three pots bubbling without any fire. One of the pots turns things into copper, the second into silver, and the third into gold. He also finds a young girl, the Master Maid. They fall in love and the Master Maid helps the prince finish three impossible tasks by teaching him the right tricks. The happy couple tries to escape from the giant. The Master Maid drops three drops of blood that respond back to the giant when he tries to check on them during his sleep. When the giant wakes up and pursues them. The Master Maid throws a lump of salt to create a mountain to block the giant, then a flask of water to create a sea to prevent the giant from pursuing them.

When the prince goes to his castle to arrange for a grand entry of the Master Maid, a witch throws a spell so he forgets about her. She finds an old hut to live in. Three suitors try to woo her, but she has them glued with her magic to different objects, the first to a poker, the second to a door knob, and the third to the tail of a calf. All three can only escape after a night of trials.

When the prince sets out to marry the evil

witch, the carriage breaks down and the Master Maid's poker, door and calf are used to repair the carriage. When the prince invites the Master Maid to the wedding, she puts a golden apple and two golden chickens on the table. The chickens start fighting over the apple and the Master Maid reminds the prince that the chickens are fighting hard just as they were fighting hard to escape the giant. The prince remembers the escapade and marries the Master Maid instead of the witch.

In this story, there are several magical objects, the vats that boil without fire, the drops of blood that respond back to the giant, the magical objects that help them escape and the magical objects to which the suitors get glued.

Among these objects, we have already discussed how to create the magical objects that thwart the pursuing giant in the chapter on the Prince of Vardhaman. In this chapter, let us look at the other magical objects in the story.

Fireless Pots of Metal

A pot, that can boil without a fire underneath and converts anything dipped into it into a metal, may appear like magic to the ancient Norwegian. However, if you recall a bit of High School Science, it will become a rather easy

61

affair to create something of that nature today.

If you recall the basic elements of electroplating, each of these vats can be realized as an electroplating system, coating elements inserted into them with copper, silver or gold respectively. A typical electroplating system does not require a burning fire, but an electric current to pass through it. The vat would contain a solution of a salt of the metal, and one of the electrodes will contain bar of the metal. The item to be electroplated will become the other electrode through which electricity will be passed.

With an electric current passing through the vat, it would bubble and boil without any fire underneath, and satisfy all the requirements of the magical story. Electroplating kits for home science projects are readily available today, and can readily provide the magical vat at home.

Talking Drops of Blood

The talking drops of blood can be created with modern processors without requiring any blood at all. The drops basically listen for the question from the giant who asks "Is the stew ready?" In response, the drops reply "Not yet" for the first two times, and they reply "Yes, it is ready" the third time.

62

A system that can listen to human voice and give an intelligent response is demonstrated by Apple Siri[15], Amazon Echo[16] and Google Home[17] in many houses today. All that we need to do is to program one such speaker to respond in the right way to the requests being spoken to.

With the flexibility provided by the modern computers, speech processing systems and web-accessible services like IBM Watson[18], we can program a simple computer (e.g. a Raspberry Pi) or an old Smartphone to respond to the queries of the giant. As a matter of fact, we can program the system to respond to the giant in a more sophisticated manner than what the Master Maid did.

Of course, the Master Maid was in a hurry to elope with the prince, and you can excuse her for only delaying the giant with three responses. Or perhaps she was timing it so that the magical lump of salt and the flask of water can be used at the right opportunity. We can only guess.

---

[15] https://www.apple.com/ios/siri/
[16] https://www.amazon.com/Amazon-Echo-Bluetooth-Speaker-with-WiFi-Alexa
[17] https://madeby.google.com/home/
[18] https://www.ibm.com/watson/

Magical Sticky Objects

How can we create magical objects like the door-knob, the poker and the tail of the horse to which a person can get stuck?

If you have read the warning on some bottles of glue which warn that it bonds skin instantly, the non-magical approach to get people stuck to those objects is relatively trivial. If those objects were coated with the right type of glue, the person holding on to them would get bonded to them instantly.

Glues made from cyano-acrylate monomers have the property that they can become polymers in the presence of moisture. A monomer is a small molecule, while a polymer is a chain consisting of several molecules. The cyano-acrylate monomers form polymers very quickly, and they make everything around them stick very strongly. The moisture present in human skin triggers the glue to bond and stick well.

Depending on the specific type of glue used, the bond can be fairly strong and hold for some time. When one accidentally gets glue on one's hand, the advice is to try to get unstuck slowly and gradually and use some chemical like acetone to dissolve the glue. However, if you

64

are a panicked suitor who is trying to jerk the hand away, you are more likely to get more glue onto other parts of your hand and get stuck even faster.

So, it appears like the magic in fairy tale of *Master Maid* can be recreated relatively easily with modern technology. Any smart girl can achieve all that the Master Maid did with access to the proper tools and chemicals.

Nevertheless, it would be safe to avoid entering the services of any cannibalistic giant, no matter how much technology you have at your disposal.

Other Fairy Tales

Talking objects that help the hero are found in many fairy tales. In this story, the drops of blood respond back to the giant in place of the maid. In *La Belle Eulalie*, (a French Fairy tale), Eulalie bakes two pies which respond back to her father, the devil, to let her escape with the hero. In *King Kojata*, (a Russian fairy tale), the heroine breathes on the window, and the frost answers for her when she is addressed. In the Polish version of King Kojata, the heroine spits on the ground and the spit answers back for her. All these talking magic objects can be realized with current technology.

The Three Spinners

The Three Spinners is a German fairy tale in which a lazy girl is scolded by her mother for not doing anything. When the queen overhears her and asks for an explanation, the mother does not want to admit that her daughter is lazy. Instead she claims that the daughter is spinning flax so fast that she can't afford to buy things.

The queen is impressed and brings the girl over with her, asking her to spin a room full of flax. The girl does not do anything until she is visited by three deformed spinners, one with a big foot, one with a big thumb and the third with a big lip. They offer to spin the entire flax if the girl will invite them to her wedding party.

When the girl consents, she goes off to sleep and the entire flax is spun very quickly. The queen decides to marry the girl to her son, and the deformed women come to the party. When the queen asks for the reason behind their deformities, they say it happened due to spinning too much. Dismayed by this, the queen forbids her new daughter-in-law from spinning, and the daughter lives happily ever after with her new husband.

The magic in this fairy tale is that of a system

that can spin a roomful of flax very rapidly. This system can be implemented without too much difficulty with modern technology. As for the deformed women, deformities exist in real people due to a variety of medical conditions and need no magical explanation.

Mechanized spinning machines can spin flax (or any other material) much faster than a single human can, and with a much better quality. Even simple spinning machines, e.g. the spinning jenny that was invented around 1770, could improve the speed of spinning very rapidly. One person can spin with a jenny as much yarn as 20-100 could spin using the previous technology of a spinning wheel.[19] Spinning a room full of flax within a few hours would be relatively easy with a spinning jenny.

Now consider a spinning jenny which is not operated by a human but by a computer. Such a jenny would be even faster and easily produce the work of a 1000 workers. Spinning a roomful of flax would be trivial using modern machinery.

Spinning today is done in factories and thus

---

[19] The Invention of the Spinning Machines, in Great Inventors and their Inventions, by Frank Bachman.

the computerized spinning machines targeted for an individual are not likely to be appearing commercially for a while. Nevertheless, spinning huge amounts of flax in a very little amount of time will not be considered very magical in modern times.

There are many fairy tales with similar stories of a magical being who can spin huge amounts of flax in no time at all. The German tale of *Rumpeltstiltskin*, the Norwegian tale of *The Three Aunts*, and the Italian tale of *And Seven,* all rely on a magical being that can spin amazing quantities with incredible quality of resulting yarn. Mechanized systems are the technological equivalents which can make any normal human perform this magical feat.

Aladdin

The story of Aladdin is one of the better-known stories from the Arabian Nights. It tells the story of a poor boy who comes across a stranger claiming to be his uncle. The stranger takes Aladdin to a remote area where his magic spells and a fire reveal a trap-door leading to an underground hole. The magician gives him a magic ring to protect him against the magic in the hole, ordering him to bring him a lamp. Aladdin gets the lamp, but refuses to give it to the stranger until he is pulled out of the hole. In the ensuing argument, the stranger shuts the cave with his magic spell. Aladdin discovers that the ring and the lamp are both magical. The ring controls a genie that can move people anywhere. The lamp summons a much more powerful genie, who provides Aladdin with foods, jewels, builds a grand castle overnight, and can also move that castle across great distances with no effort.

The rest of the story deals with Aladdin's adventures with these magic objects, how he uses them to marry the princess of the land, and outwits the pretend uncle who returned to trick the princess to gain control of the lamp.

There are three magical objects in the story,

the magic ring, the magic lamp, and the magical trap-door. Let us see how we can create these magic objects, or their close approximation with present day technology.

Magic Ring

The magic ring is a device which produces a genie that enables a person to move from one place to another. The movement of the genie includes the ability to rescue a person from a closed space.

The genie of the magic lamp is summoned by means of rubbing the ring. You talk to the genie to express where you want to be transported, and the genie then does the needful.

If you are one of the many people who are used to wearable devices such as smart watches, you can easily imagine a ring be created which incorporates a processor, a network interface, a speaker, a microphone and a projection display. The projection display will project the image of a genie which will show itself on the first wall or surface which the projected light encounters. The genie then will be visible only when the person is inside, or next to some surface outside. However, the person can interact with the ring/genie at any location.

70

The ring can then be viewed simply as a user interface device that can fetch a device to move people from one place to another. If you are outside, the ring can communicate over the network with a remote system, e.g. a personal airplane and ask it to come over to the location that you are at.

For those who are used to ordering taxis or ride-sharing services using a mobile application on their Smartphone, the experience is not far from that of the genie of the magic ring. You express your desire of the destination, a car appears in a few minutes, and whisks you away to wherever you desire to be. If you replace the taxi operated by a driver with a self-driving car, or a self-flying drone, you have the genie who can move you by magic between any two points that are drivable (self-driving cars) or reachable via air (personal airplane).

What if you are trapped indoors or underground like Aladdin. There is no restriction that the ring be used to control just a car or a plane. You can imagine the ring sending a command to a central location which contains an assortment of robotic devices, including but not limited to self-driving cars, robots that can open trapdoors to underground cellars, self-flying personal airplanes, robots with an

71

assortment of master keys so they can open locks etc.

The user interface (genie) of the magic ring learns your desired destination, and knows your current location (e.g. using GPS signals assuming you are not in a place that completely blocks any feasible way of knowing your position), it can work out a plan that can bring you out. A robot can come along with the self-driving car to open any doors that may be keeping you locked inside, and similarly get you to any location which you want to be in.

Magic Lamp

The magic lamp is a user-interface just like the magic ring. It is also activated when one rubs on it (e.g. when one swipes on the touch-screen of a Smartphone), and reveals a genie who can talk with you to get your desires.

The genie will bring you food, jewelry or other items that you desire. If you have an online shopping account with any of the retailers, you can use a mobile application (or a few clicks on a browser) to get the same functionality today.

All that you need to convert that into an experience with the genie of the magic lamp is a device shaped like a lamp whose outer surface is a touch-screen, and which includes a microphone/speaker and a processor to talk with you and to process your orders. In other words, you just need a phone that looks like a lamp. All that can be created today without any significant technical challenges.

The lamp can also be used to request that a castle be built overnight. Refer to the chapter on the legend of Patna to see how that may be accomplished.

The only aspect that is different from the magical lamp is that the online retailer or your credit card company eventually expects you to pay for the goods you order.

Magical Trap Door and Cave

The magical trap door is an entrance to a cave in the ground which is guarded by an opening which can be opened only by a secret magic spell. The cave consists of several shiny objects and jewels. However, until the magic lamp is taken from its stand, touching any of the objects will result in instant death. It is safe to take the objects once the magic lamp is removed from its perch.

Assuming money is no object, you can fill

any cave with gems and jewels that you like. There is not much magic in it. The magic is in having a magical spell to open the trap-door and in having the cave where anyone who has not pocketed the magic lamp will be killed if they touch any of the other jewels.

The magical spell to open the trap-door can be created today using speech recognition software which uses the secret spell as a password to allow the opening of the trap-door. The mechanism for it will be the same as that which opens the cave in the legend of *Alibaba and Forty Thieves*. We have seen how to create such a system in an earlier chapter.

A computer controlled mechanism can also be used to create the magic cave. If each of the gems/jewels is kept on a pressure-sensitive switch, i.e. removing anyone of them will send a signal to a computer, and the computer can then trigger the mechanism of death for the intruder. This mechanism can be either releasing a hail or arrow or bullets, or pick any other mechanism you can imagine.

The computer mechanism can be deactivated once the magic lamp is removed from its perch (which again can be a pressure sensitive system).

Such presume sensitive mechanism are used in the mini-bars of some hotels, where removing a can of drink from the fridge results in a computer automatically charging your room for the drink. With both the hardware and the software for the system used commercially, you can create the magic cave with the exact same characteristics as the one in which Aladdin found the magic lamp.

It may not be a smart idea to create a cave with a killing mechanism in modern life due to a variety of ethical and legal reasons. You may want to hook up the mechanism so that it just sounds a loud alarm to deter anyone from taking the gems/jewels.

The Red Ettin

The Red Ettin is a Scottish fairytale in which two brothers (or three in some versions) leave their home to seek their fortune. The older brother leaves a knife with the younger brother. The knife would be clear if the older brother is fine, but will turn dusty if the older brother comes to any harm. The older brother is not nice to an old woman he meets on the way. He comes across a herd of wild beasts and seeks refuge in a cottage. But the cottage belongs to a monster, the Red Ettin, who asks the older brother a set of riddles. When the older brother is unable to answer the riddle, the Red Ettin turns the older brother into a stone.

The younger brother sets out when he sees the knife has turned dusty. He is nice to the old woman who tells him the answer to the riddles and the secret of the Red Ettin. The younger brother also receives a magic wand which kills the wild beasts when they approach him. He answers the riddle of the Red Ettin, and kills him. He rescues the ladies captured by the Red Ettin, including the princess of Scotland, who marries the younger brother. The older brother is also restored back to flesh and blood from stone.

There are two magical objects in the story, the knife that turns dusty when the older brother is harmed, and the magic wand which kills the ferocious beasts.

Magic Wand

The magic wand that can kill the wild animals with ease could be a gun.

There is not much magic associated with a gun in the modern age. Modern guns, especially those that are semi-automatic can kill many beasts, wild or not, with a fair bit of ease.

Guns do need a bit of training to use, but we can make a reasonable assumption that the fairy (old woman) who gave the gun to the younger brother could instruct him how to use the gun, along with directions to reload it with bullets, and how to handle it safely. She probably would have also provided an adequate supply of bullets.

Perhaps guns did not exist during the time when the legend of the Red Ettin was created, but they are not very difficult to manufacture today. A man armed with a gun need not be afraid of wild animals.

Magic Knife

The magic knife indicates the health status of one brother to another. It can be created today using the various pervasive devices that are available today.

A wearable device such as a wrist-band can measure the pulse of the person, and use the pulse rate as a measure of the wellbeing of a person. If the pulse rate drops to zero, then the person is not alive (assuming the wrist-band is still being worn). If the wrist-band is connected to a network, it can relay the state of the pulse to any other device on the same network. As a simple example, the wrist-band can send an alert to a phone via a text message is it sees that the pulse rate has fallen to zero.

The magic knife is the device on the other side, i.e. the phone which would receive the alert. When it receives the alert, it displays the fact that the alert has been received. On a phone, one gets some visual pop-up when the text or alert is received. However, on the magic knife, one can use other mechanisms, specifically one that changes the color of the knife to look like a dusty one.

A simple way to change the color of the knife will be to have a small LED bulb in the handle of the knife. The bulb would emit a brownish light, or one can put a brown-colored filter on top of a bulb with white light. The bulb lights up when it receives the alert that the pulse on the wearing device has gone silent, and the knife appears to have turned dusty.

You can make a device like the knife if needed, but if you are willing to live with just an alert on a phone, you may be able to program it yourself using any common pulse monitoring wrist-bands and just have an alert be sent to the phone if the pulse shows unusual behavior.

Still Magical

The part of the story where the older brother is turned into stone by magic and restored to the flesh and blood form when the Ettin is killed is an element that modern technology has not been able to attain yet.

The Lady of Gollerus

The Lady of Gollerus is an Irish fairy tale which tells of a man called Fitzgerald who was smoking a pipe on the beach and came across a pretty maiden who had a *cohuleen driuth*, or an enchanted cap on her side. Fitzgerald steals the enchanted cap, and does not return it despite the pleas of the maiden. Instead of that, he persuades the maiden to marry him and become Mrs. Fitzgerald.

Some years into the marriage, Mrs. Fitzgerald discovers the enchanted cap when she was cleaning the house and Fitzgerald was away. She puts it back on, and goes into the sea never to return. She was a mermaid who needed the enchanted cap to go back to her people.

The *cohuleen driuth* or enchanted cap is found in other Irish legends as well. The cap is used by the mer-people who live in the sea. They can go in the sea when they have the cap, but without the cap, they are just like ordinary people on land.

With the magic of modern technology, you can walk into a store, buy the *cohuleen driuth* and use it off the shores of Ireland. However, it is highly unlikely that any modern day Irish person would consider you a magic mer-person because you show up on their shore with this enchanted cap.

The function of the *cohuleen driuth* can be performed today by means of diving helmets, gear that is used by professional sea divers. The diving helmets can be used to supply air from a scuba gear or from a surface vehicle. In order to do the job of a cap in the legend, we will have to consider the diving helmets that are designed to work with a scuba gear. To go underwater, one would need the helmet as well as the scuba gear.

One special type of diving helmet is a full-face diving mask, as shown above. The full-face diving mask provides air from the scuba gear in the back of the, and is small enough to come into the category of an enchanted cap.

So, the mysterious mer-people may just be a group of ancient people who had figured out how to dive with scuba gear and a face mask. When they showed up on the shores of ancient Ireland, they were mistaken for mer-people. After all, they appeared from the sea, and disappeared from the sea to magically appear again. The ancient Irish would have assumed that the mer-people came from some place under the sea.

The mermaid who ended up becoming Mrs. Fitzgerald might have been a young girl who took the boat alone one day to find new places to scuba dive. She surfaced on land and had the bad fortune to run into Mr. Fitzgerald. If the boat was anchored at a distance, she could not go back to her boat without the diving gear but lost no opportunity in sneaking away at the first chance she got.

The face mask would have required some scuba gear to supply the air, but she could have hidden that gear somewhere nearby. All Fitzgerald saw was the face mask (or the diving helmet) which gave rise to the legend of the *cohuleen driuth*.

Of course, the above is sheer speculation. But the enchanted cap of Irish legends is something we can all buy and use today, provided we are willing to learn diving.

The Princess on Glass Hill

The Princess on Glass Hill is a fairy tale from Norway in which a king promises to marry his daughter to the suitor who can reach her, while she is seated on the top of a glass hill. The glass hill is vertical like a wall and slippery like ice. As a result, anyone who tries to do so fails because of the slipperiness of the glass.

The youngest of three brothers in the Kingdom gets access to three horses because he was brave enough to stay guarding his father's fields while his brothers fled. The horses come with magical horse shoes and one could climb up a third of the mountain, the other one climbs up to half of the hill, and the third one climbs up to the entire top. The youngest brother marries the princess.

Let us see how well we can recreate the task of fitting a horse with shoes that will let it climb up a slippery glass hill.

Magical Horse Shoe

If one has to climb up a really slippery surface like a glass wall, one of the techniques that can be used is that of suction cups. The fact that suction cups can be used to scale a glass wall was demonstrated in a prominent world-

84

wide news event in August of 2016, when a protestor tried to scale the Trump Tower in New York[20]. The climber used suction cups to climb up the large glass windows of Trump tower. They were powerful enough to hold the weight on one person safely against the surface.

In principle, one can attach suction cups at the bottom of a horse-shoe, and use that to have the horse scale the side of a glass mountain. One major challenge in this design is that the glass surface needs to be very smooth in order for suction cups to work. Suction cups won't work very well on non-glass surfaces or when the glass is coarse. In order to apprehend the climber of the Trump Tower, the police in New York removed glass panes from the windows of the building, and compelled the climber towards a location where they could reach out and grab him for an arrest.

Even if we assume that the climbing has to be done on a very smooth glass surface where suction cups would work well, we still face another challenge. In order to support the weight of a person, the suction cups need to be really

---

[20]   http://time.com/4447369/man-scales-trump-tower-suction-cups/

large. Furthermore the person needs to climb in a posture where the body and the center of gravity stay close to the surface of the wall. The climber using suction cups is essentially crawling up the wall, trying to minimize the distance between the wall and its body. A person mounted on the horse is at a fair bit of distance away from the glass wall.

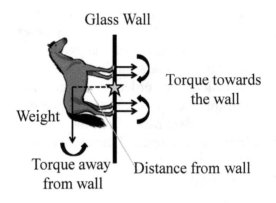

Basic physics dictates why it is better to climb in a position close to the surface. If you recall the basic principles of force and torque from high school physics, the weight of a horse will be a force through its center of gravity, and cause a torque pulling the person away from the glass wall, while the suction cups will cause a torque keeping the person attached to the wall. Torque is the product of force and distance around a point. The further the center of gravity is away from the wall, the higher the torque will be pulling the person away from the wall. The figure above shows the torques around the point marked with a star. With a rider mounted on the horse, the torque pulling away from the wall will be even larger. By staying close to the wall, the human climber can reduce this torque, but a horse cannot be expected to do the same.

If this sounds like a difficult challenge, we need not be disheartened yet. There are a few more technologies that can be used to scale a slippery glass hill. These are technologies that can provide a larger suction force than the suction cup.

The Defense Advanced Research Projects Agency (DARPA) is an agency of the U.S. government which sponsors development of new technology. In a program called Z-man[21] operational in 2010s, it explored development of new types of adhesive substances which would allow soldiers to scale up vertical walls without ropes or ladders. The program turned up new

---

[21] http://www.darpa.mil/program/z-man

technologies, some of them inspired by animals like geckos that can climb up vertical surfaces with ease.

The secret to gecko's climbing is in the structure of its feet. It consists of millions of tiny hairs which end in really tiny endpoints. These microscopic hair end-points result in causing an attractive force (like a really small suction cup) against the wall. These microscopic attractive forces are called Van-der-Waal's forces. They are named after a Dutch scientist who lived in the early 19th century, and developed the theory of molecular science. Several theoretical equations in Physics including the force behind gecko's feet are named after this amazing scientist, who began his career as a school teacher. He learnt physics on his own and went on to win the Nobel Prize in physics for his work.

Scientists from several universities and companies working on the DARPA project were able to exploit the secret of gecko's feet to build adhesive surfaces that could provide an amazing adhesive force. A square patch of 4 inches on each side (an area of 16 square inches) could hold an object weighing 660 pounds. Four horse shoes on the four feet of a horse could support a weight of 2500 pounds. Given that an average light horse would weigh around 1000 pounds, we can start to imagine horse-shoes made out of such adhesive surfaces that can hold a horse against a glass wall.

The DARPA program also showed the technical feasibility of surfaces that used microscopic hooks that will fit into a vertical surface and provide an ability to climb other types of surfaces. Those surfaces can help climb walls that may not exactly be clean, or be made up of materials other than glass.

Horse shoes made from such sticky surfaces can make the fairy tale of the princess on the glass hill come true. The challenge of actually training a horse to overcome its fears and actually climb up a wall would need to be sorted out. We could speculate that the three horses were able to climb up part of the distance depending on the training available to them.

Other Fairy tales

There are a couple of other fairy tales which have a glass hill or glass mountain which need to be scaled. There is a Polish fairy tale called *The Glass Mountain* where golden apples grow on top of a glass mountain. A boy kills a lynx and uses its claws to scale up the mountain. It is attacked by an eagle but the boy hangs onto the eagle's feet to reach the top of the mountain. The apples cure all the injuries of the boy and he gets to marry the princess who was enchanted to live on the glass mountain.

Modern technology can create the claws from gecko's feet, and a boy may indeed be better able to scale up the glass wall than someone trying to climb up a glass hill on horseback. The golden apples which can cure any injury instantly, however, will remain magical with the current state of technology available to us.

The Giant without a Heart

The Giant without a Heart is a Norwegian fairy tale in which a roaming prince comes across the castle of a giant in which a pretty princess is being kept as a captive. The princess falls in love with the prince, and the prince wants to kill the giant to rescue the princess. However, the giant cannot be killed because his heart in not in the body. The heart is kept outside the body in a secret location.

The princess tricks the giant into revealing the location of the heart. The prince finds the heart, and destroys it resulting in the death of the giant. There are many other nuances in the fairy tale, and the difficulties encountered by the prince in finding the heart, but the main magical component is a giant who cannot die until the remotely separated heart is destroyed.

Won't it be fun to create a giant who is invincible and cannot be destroyed because its heart is somewhere else?

The Mechanical Giant

The giant is a large person who will survive any attack as long as its heart, which is outside its body, is not damaged. However, when the heart is destroyed, the giant would be destroyed.

If we have to have a giant that cannot be damaged in any other way other than by destroying its heart, it is reasonable to assume that the body of the giant is made not of flesh but from some metal. It can also be made from a plastic or any other hard material that will be difficult to destroy.

Several humanoid robots are available on the market today, but most of them look like mechanical toys than a human being. However, it is possible to create robots that look like a human being, where the skin looks like realistic human skin, with sufficient number of controls on the muscle to create expressions like smiles, and a natural conversation, and limbs driven by tendons that approach realistic human movement.

At present, most of the robots, regardless of how human-like they look, are controlled using a processor which is usually embedded within the robot. This allows the robot to move about, while the controller guides its movement, and responds back to the stimuli it receives from the environment. The robot processor would run Artificial Intelligence software, which can allow it to hold a conversation, interpret the scenes around it as it scans the surface, and with the advent of new technologies for sensing chemicals in the air, can even create an electronic nose. With an electronic nose and a computer generated voice, the artificial mechanic can easily remark –"I smell a human," or whatever other equivalent comments giants make in different variations of the fairy tale.

Assuming that the processor is the heart of the giant, we can consider a slightly modified design where the processor that controls the operations of the mechanical giant is not embedded inside the robot, but is connected via a wireless network to a remote device. In modern Internet-connected world, the remote processor can be anywhere. It could be another system running half-way across the globe; all that it needs is a network connecting it to the robot.

Some of the functions of a mechanical giant may need to be performed within a fraction of a millisecond, e.g. the controls that make it walk smoothly or help it lift something using its hands. The software to control those functions can be in a processor that is embedded within the mechanical giant. The software that does not need to respond with the same rapid responsiveness e.g. responding back to a spoken command which appears spontaneously if it is completed within 100 milliseconds (approx) can be on the remote processor.

Having a remote processor also provides fault tolerance to the mechanical robot. The robot will not die as long as the remote processor is up and active. Even if the robot is attacked, the remote processor can restart the local processor and can be programmed to perform repairs on any limbs that have been damaged. These can include the ability to replace the local processor in case it is damaged. The local processor can be dual or triple redundant, so that even if one fails, the others can take over, and perform the required repairs to replace the defective processor.

While it will be fairly expensive and require a significant mechanical design and software programming, the technologies to build a robot that looks like a human (or a giant human) and is controlled by a remote processor is technically feasible.

And if you really want to remain true to the story, you can package the hardware containing the remote processor into a system that looks like a heart.

Other Fairy Tales

There are several other fairy tales in which a

magical creature is invincible and can only be destroyed if some remote object is destroyed. All of those magical creatures can be viewed as an instance of the mechanical giant described earlier, with variations in the shape used by the mechanical robot, and the remote processor.

In the Serbian fairy tale of *The Dragon and the Prince*, the mechanical monster is a dragon that talks, and the remote processor is in a pigeon. Once the pigeon is destroyed, the dragon dies.

In the Scottish legend of *The Sea-Maiden*, the sea-maiden is a mermaid whose life is in an egg. The sea-maiden is destroyed when the egg is killed. We can make the mechanical robot is the shape of a mermaid, and the remote processor in the shape of an egg. As long as the internal processors and software are similar, the same design would work to replicate the magical creature.

In the Portuguese fairy tale of *What comes of Picking Flowers*, the heroine is kidnapped by a monster who can only be killed when a particular egg is smashed against its head. The monster is the mechanical robot, and egg is the remote processor is an egg.

In another Scottish tale, *The Young King of Easaidh Ruadh*, which is also known as *The King of the Waterfalls*, we find another giant whose life is stored in a remote egg.

In the Irish fairy tale of *The Three Daughters of King O'Hara,* the roles of the male and female characters are reversed. In this story, the evil person is a queen who is forcing the groom of the youngest princess to marry her. The evil queen can only be killed by destroying an egg.

In all of these tales, the remote device holds the life and strength of the evil monster (or giant or mermaid). With modern technology, such evil monsters whose life is outside their body can be created.

Of course, it is hard to think of a good reason to create such a giant.

List of Fairy Tales

The list below enumerates various fairy tales, legends, or myths which mention some magical objects which can be attained with modern technology.